LOVE,
SEX,
ROMANCE
& OTHER
BAD THINGS

LOVE, SEX, ROMANCE & OTHER BAD THINGS

A Collection of Poetry
and Spoken Word

PJ

PHOENIX JAMES

LOVE, SEX, ROMANCE & OTHER BAD THINGS

First Edition: 2022

ISBN: 978-1-7397925-0-3 (Paperback)
ISBN: 978-1-7397925-1-0 (Ebook)

Cover Artwork & Design by Phoenix James.
Book Design & Formatting by Phoenix James.

Visit the author's website at www.PhoenixJamesOfficial.com or email him at phoenix@PhoenixJamesOfficial.com

DEDICATION

To all who came before me
To all who made me possible
To all who made me worthy
And to all who come this way
I hope this pleases you

And to a young boy
Who began this journey
A long time ago

Thank you for the breadcrumbs
They helped me find my way

I hope I haven't let you down
I hope you're proud.

CONTENTS

ABOUT TO HAVE SEX

We're just about to have sex
My body part hard and erect
Hers stimulated and wet
She's breathing heavily
Beginning to break into a sweat
I want to push it inside
But she's not quite ready yet
She wants to savour the flavour
Of my sweet caress
As I massage her breast
And between her legs
The bed
Becomes our playground of foreplay
Exploring
Whilst touching
With nothing to say
Just deep breaths
And whispers
Of fulfilment
Joy and ecstasy
I had been yearning for so long
To get with her
She too had been yearning
To get with me

And learning her curves
Seemed to come
So naturally and easily
I had dreamt of her
Many times before
Actually
Previously we kissed
But never like this
Usually it was just on the cheek
The way friends greet
When they meet
But now we're in bed
Naked beneath the sheets
I'm laying between her legs
She's kissing my neck
And I'm caressing her breasts
So wantonly and lustfully
It's been a long time coming
We can't help but express
In excess
No contemplating what's next
We're just about
To have sex.

ALRIGHT NOW

I always brought you breakfast
In the morning
Up before the break of dawn
And it was just to please you
Brought you flowers
And sweet kisses
In the evening
Always called you
In the afternoon
Just to see that you were okay
And if you wanted me to bring anything
Home from work that day
Took you out to fancy restaurants
Took care of all your needs
And all your wants
We used to take walks
In the park
In the summer time
We used to do a whole lot of things
We don't do anymore
And you know why
I can't stand
To be around a woman
Who's just so untrue

I've got to move on
I'm leaving you
I've got to find me a woman
Who wouldn't run out on me
Just one good lady
Who lives honestly

And I'll be alright
I'll be alright

It's just one o clock
In the morning
And I've just finished
Packing my bags for me to leave
I waited for you
So I could explain before I go
But now
It's a quarter past three
So I wrote you this letter
And by the time you read it
I'll be on the other side of town
I know this way
Things can only be better
Most definitely
Without you around
Telling me all kinds of stories

4

That I know are lies
About why you stayed out
So late last night
Thought I gave you everything
And was the best that I could be
Gave you all the love
But it was obvious to see
That you'd rather be with him
Than to be with me
Girl, I was so sorry
I had to set you free

But I'm alright
I'm alright now

Now you're ringing me
On my phone
Saying you want me to come home
Saying sorry you treated me that way
And you were just so very afraid
That I would hurt you
And then go away
And that you really hope it's not too late
Because you are making a pact
Right here today
To never leave me

And never go astray
By my side
You promise to stay
Every night
And every day
In each and every
God given way
No matter what the people say
You'll be there

But I'm never coming back
To your promises
And lies

Because I'm alright
I'm alright now.

ANOTHER LOVE

It's been so long now
Since you knocked upon my door
Well, well
If it's love you're looking for
You won't find it here anymore
Because I gave you all my loving, babe
But it wasn't enough for you to stay

I've found another love
And she's turned my life around

First it was us
Then it was you and him
Well now it's me
And my new lover
So my heart won't let you in
Girl
I hope you learn something from this
That a heart
Is not to play with

I've found another love
And she's turned my life around

Sometimes
We think we're right
When we're all so wrong
And we don't realise
Until what we had
Is gone
Sometimes
We have to bear the pain
To realise love
Is more than just a game

I've found another love
And she's turned my life around.

ARE YOU THERE YET?

Are you a treasure
Or just a trophy
Are you a nice to have
Or a necessity

Are you the text message
Or the phone call
Are you making an effort
Or none at all

Are you a date night
Or just a late night
Are you the postcard
Or the plane flight

Are you a roller coaster
Or just a bike ride
Are you a mind blower
Or just a nice time

Are you closer now
Or just between the sheets
Are you making actual love
Or make believe

Do you ever question it
Or just accept it
Do you offer it
Or just expect it

Are you the main course
Or the side dish
Does it empower you
Or just impoverish

Are you doing it
Or just on the to do list
Are you the go for it
Or the I wish

Are you a make it happen
Or a wait and see
Are you a definite
Or a supposed to be.

ASIAN GIRL CRIES

Life's deep
I think to myself
As I watch
A young Asian girl cry
Tears rolling from her eyes
We never got to speak
Otherwise
I could've asked her why
It's almost as if
I felt her pain inside
But I am left to wonder why
This young Asian girl cries
I saw her receive
No phone call
No news
From a passer by
No incident I could see
That I could instantly
Relate to her life
Possibly a thought
Brought only to her mind
One I could not see
One that she herself
May have experienced

At an earlier time
Still I wonder why
This young Asian girl cries
In my head
I try to guess
The reason
For her distress
Could it be the love of a man
Which once was
But now suddenly left
Could that be the reason?
A love
Who has simply lost interest
Or highly religious
Caring but overbearing parents
Who protest
For her
They want only the best
Nevertheless
She departs
With tears
Still streaming from her eyes
And I am left
To wonder still
Why
This young Asian girl cries.

BREAK AWAY

Tell me something
About yourself
Something known
By no-one else
That little secret
That you choose to hide
That special something
You keep deep inside
Break away

The time is now
For you and I
To let it go
So we can fly
Break away

Time to be
All that we can be
Push pride aside
And let your heart be free
There's so much more
To life
For you and me
So enjoy the ride
And just let it be
Break away.

COMFORTABLE MYSTERY

Two fleeting lovers in the night
Embrace in a kiss
Seduced by a romantic melody
Perform before a rich man
Who takes pleasure in their presence
Caressing a warm and willing guitar
A footbridge
Planted underneath our feet
We too soak in the beauty of the city
Our eyes dance
Across a mischievous river
Drawn in by the allure
All the pretty little night lights
Overlooking
Co-conspirators in the whole affair
We capture what catches us
Taken up in all of this mystery.

DIFFERENCES

I liked the peace and quiet
You liked the riot
I wanted to gain weight
You were on a diet
You like the daylight
I liked the stars in the darkness
You said you wanted to finish it
When I just got started
You liked white wine
I preferred the cherry
You liked it with ice cream
I preferred the jelly
You walked with your girls
I often walked alone
You'd go out to the nightclub
I'd stay in and write a poem
You loved to fuck
I liked to make love
I preferred the slow touch
You couldn't get enough
I thought I was pretty easy-going
You complained how much I moaned
But since we finished
I'm beginning to like our differences
Let's make this a happy home.

FEEL

Was beginning to feel cursed
Wasted
Losing faith in relationships
But then
The police can only escort a man
Away from the home of his children
So many times
Before he starts to feel that way
About shit
Thinking in my soul
I know there has to be much better
Than this
And sitting in that prison cell
Long enough
Can also play mind tricks
I mean
How many times
Can a man stand
A woman disrespecting his mother
On her own doorstep
Before he flips
Or how many times
Will he refrain
From just turning up

And breaking the door down
When she says no
You can't see your kids
Disturbing the peace
But where is the peace
In keeping a father from his child
And a child from its dad
Especially when a mother knows
That's something she can't give
Not to mention
Something she herself
May have never even had
But too often
When a woman feels hurt
When a woman feels scorned
What baby might need and feel
Ain't really the real issue at hand
It's more like what is the best weapon
I have to hurt this man
Like he hurt me
How dare he leave me
Don't care if he loves his child
He ain't going to see this baby
And there's me
Young 23
Wild and crazy

Dusting off my fatigues
And dessert boots
From my solo expedition
Egyptian sun still in my braids
Skin glistening
Nile water
Still in my system
Four years down the road
Virginia heat can't compare
And what I've been envisioning
Is clear
As I'm repositioning
Sitting in your passenger seat
And sweetness
I don't think you're listening
When I say
I'm a stranger here
That I have never felt like this
You came out of nowhere
Unknowingly
Restoring my faith in relationships
And I know we've both had our fair share
Of crazy shit
That's how I know
Exactly how this feels for you
When you say

You're scared of disappointment
But nothing is certain
And our tomorrow
Is not promised
So let's just share the enjoyment
And to be honest
I've been looking forward
To today
Us being here
Together again
You are an extraordinary person
I see myself in you
I feel like you understand me
And I want us
To be more than friends
And I don't care
If that might sound cliché
But these
Are some of the things
I've been only waiting to say
Since our date
On the train
On the bus
At the show
How do I explain
To a woman

I really barely even know
That I can hear
And read her pain
That I'm beginning to believe
There's more
To our connection
And it's real
How do I too
Let go of the fear
And the pride
Of all the layers
And the lies
To tell you
This
Is how I feel.

FORMER ADVANCES

Now to start with
Her former advances
Seemed harmless
At least
That's what I thought
Until it started
I mean
Innocent thoughts
Became tarnished
By
If I take my chances
Judging by how intimate
This dance is
Chance is
I could enchant this
Brown skin
Sexy thing
Home to my advantage
That I could enhance this
From dance floor darkness
To a candle lit bliss
And that if I play my cards right
I can't miss

I don't usually do it
On the first night

But all I can envision
Is her hips
Gyrating
To the rhythm
Of my lips
And my tongue
As it licks
The sweet bitterness
From her clitoris
As she comes

I don't usually do it
On the first night

But I swear
I would savour the flavour
Of her warm wetness
Until daylight
And my bet is
A cross between
Passion fruit and honey
Is just what she tastes like
Funny

I don't usually do it
On the first night

But her former advances
Though ever so slight
Have inspired thoughts of her
Naked
Splayed atop my face
As I lie with my arms
Wrapped around her thighs
As I taste
And lick
And lick
And suck
And drink her fine juices down
Until the sun comes up
And for a while there
We remain
Tucked up
No questions asked
No need to explain
And I just slip down
And suck
From her luscious tasting sugar cane
All over again
Her former advances

Go backwards and forwards
Spinning around inside my brain
While the DJ spins
And another song plays
As we graciously exchange names
I'm thinking
I hope my thinking
Is not in vain
Thinking
I hope her thoughts
Are the same.

FORMER ADVANCES II

I don't usually do it
On the first night
But here I am
Transfixed
In this moment in time again
Behind my eyes again
Inside my mind again
Between her thighs again
And I'm tasting her
Like the pleasures all mine again
And for every breath I take
She takes four
And for every sound she makes
I want more
More than I can imagine
My face immersed
Inside her warm wet cavern of passion
Enjoying the flavour of her nature
Bathing my face
In the juice
That constitutes her essence
And as we dance
She holds me closer
And I can feel more of her presence

Wondering if she can hear
What I am thinking about
Doing sexy things
To her down south
With my mouth
And if she can
I'm shameless
After all
She made the first advance
And judging by the way
She's kissing on my neck
This is more
Than just a dance
And that's cool
Because if like me
She's single again
And ready to mingle again
And meet new friends again
And if the vibe between us
At the end of the night is right
Then I'm more than ready
To leave this club
And head to a more
Intimate location
Have sex
Or make love

Or just conversation
Let me see
I'm young
I like to have fun
And do freaky things with my tongue
Until women cum
Here I am
Thinking myself into a situation
That she may not even
Have a remote interest in
Not to mention
I've overheard so many women say
It's just a dance
But based on her actions
And the energy she's giving off
That's not what she's suggesting
Not in the way she's holding
And stroking me
And still kissing
And sucking on my neck
And with the same energy and passion
She lustfully bites my ear
And tells me
I'm making her wet
And inside my head
I'm thinking

How good can it get
And that with the same energy
And passion
I'm going to kiss
And suck
And lick
Everything and every drop
Until there's nothing left
Or until she tells me to stop
But that's only
If she grants me the opportunity tonight
To peel her out of this sexy dress
And to make her hot
Real hot
Hotter than we both feel right now
On this crowded dance floor
But if not
Then it's her loss
But if I don't ask
I won't know
In fact I'm sure
Inside my doubting mind
That she is feeling equally as freaky
And what's more
She was the one
Who first came seeking me

With these former advances of hers
It's funny
How even as a poet
I sometimes can't find the words
To say
But hey
Today
For what it's worth
I better find a way
To express to her
These thoughts inside my head
If I don't
I may forfeit the chance
Of having her naked
Inside my bed
But in this intimate dance
So much has already been said
So what more is there really left to say
With a feeling between us so strong
As the DJ plays on
Playing another one
Of our favourite songs
And all I want
Is her open
Open wide
As I press her closer

And slide my hand
Down her waist
Towards her behind
She holds me even tighter
As if to say
She likes it and it's fine
Our bodies intertwine
And move in motion to the music
And everything feels so right
She moves her lips
Close to my ear again
And says
I liked your performance earlier
Your words that you said on the mic
And I'm really enjoying
The way we're dancing
And the way you're making me feel
And I want us to go home together
If that's alright
She said
Whatever happens
I want you to know
One thing
I don't usually
Do it
On the first night.

FUCK YOU / UGLY

How quickly
These things change
How fast it all turns
From lovey-dovey
To strange
We used to talk
Have fun and laugh all day
And play games
Now I can't even stand your fucking name
You just really rub me the wrong way
So I'm over here on my fuck you today
Why did I even fuck you anyway
You're a barefaced liar
You're vain
You're lazy
You're selfish
Your manners are bad
Your attitude stinks
Your morals are shitty
Fuck
Like you aren't even pretty
And your body is not all that
I lied
Let's face it

In fact
You as a whole
On a scale of 1-10
I'd say you're below a 5
Basic
But with that said
You're off the richter scale
When it comes to ugly
Cold and heartless
The type to always start shit
Dark hearted
No soul
You'd sell your friends
If it helped you hit your goal
Slit a persons throat
If it got your kid a vote for a TV show
You're actually the worst person I know
Absolutely no compassion for no-one
None
Lord knows
I never liked your fashion
I never liked your clothes
I never liked your mother
I never liked your sisters
I never liked your bros
All no good bad seeds

Where nothing but weed grows
People say
The fruit doesn't fall far from the tree
Well you're rotten
You and your whole family
Your teeth are ugly
Your hands are ugly
Your feet are ugly
You can't cook
You can't fuck
You can't suck
You can't kiss
And I never had the heart
To tell you
That your breath stinks
If you say that's bad
You should hear what your other exes think
And if you say anything at all
You should say it with breath mints
How the fuck
Did I ever
Get in any entanglement with you
A major lapse in fucking judgment
That'll do
It's the truth
Let's admit it

With me
You were punching
Way above your weight
And that ugly
Dumb ass
Lying
Cheating man you've been seeing
Yeah him
He's great
Perfect for you
You look good together
And as ugly as he is on the outside
He surely can't be any worse of a person
Than you
You two really suit
I'm fucking over the moon
To find out
That child
Wasn't mine too
My intelligent sperm
Surely all died
At the thought
Of living inside you
You're the devil's spawn
And anyone who knows you
Knows it

34

Your every action
And your whole energy shows it
Who doesn't know you as a hoe
Knows you as a bitch
Had to let you go like a hot potato
Quick
And find someone better
I can grow with
Someone loyal I can invest my time in
And trust
You're a fucking disloyal
Untrustworthy waste of time
So that's not you, honey
Someone kinder
Someone nicer
Someone lovely
That's definitely not you, boo
So goodbye
So long
Good luck and fuck you, ugly
Forget you
I'm done
Trust me
I'm not sweating you
Fuck you
And your dumb internet friends too.

HER SECRET RENDEZVOUS

After dark
She leaves on a journey
In pursuit of love
She feels the lust she receives at home
Is never enough
The man she leaves
Asleep at home each night
Is the man she feels
Isn't loving her right
So she ventures out
Towards a secret rendezvous
Somewhere between the hours
Of twelve and two
Wrapped in a Persian scarf
To conceal her face
There's never anyone around
But she wears it just in case
Down the back road
Towards the alley
Where it's empty
Taking no chances
She already takes plenty
She would have no excuse
For being out this time

You're either having an affair
Or you're committing crime
That's what Mrs Netcher used to say
Making jokes about the sisters
Coming home from church
Back in the day
But this is far from any fellowship
Or prayer meeting she's receiving
It's very deceiving
How she often makes plans
For the kids
In the evening
Just so she can meet him
So they can be together
For a few stolen moments
Down at the depot
He drives the number nineteen bus
So that's where she goes
To secretly make arrangements
With him
For the following night
She always takes the long way around
To avoid his wife
Who works in the bakery
On the corner of D'Arblay Street
During the week

And she'd ask too many questions
So it's better if they didn't meet
She still keeps a letter
She wrote for him
Concealed in a make-up case
Inside her bag
Describing how he makes her feel
And all the fun they have
Last week they spent the day
At an amusement park
It was out of the area
So they went in his car
Now some people
Would ask me
How I know
About her secret rendezvous
In such detail
And so precise
Well the answer is simple
Trust me
I know
She's my wife.

I HAVEN'T THOUGHT ABOUT SEX IN A WHILE

I haven't thought about sex in a while
Wild I know
But true
To tell the truth
I haven't even thought about you
It would be a lie
If I said I thought about your smile
Or the things we used to do
At least not in the way
You'd love me to
I always seem to end up
Right back here in this stuff
Feeling like I didn't make it clear enough
That I'm never really making love
As much as I'm sincerely fucking up
The smart ones run a mile
The smarter ones
Two or three
Once they come to decide
That just one of them
Is no match for two of me
Me and all of my seasons
Your reasons for not believing

You and all of your demons
Fighting to shadow box with mine
You naked wearing all of my semen
And me in nothing more than a good time
But I haven't thought about sex in a while
And the thought of that makes me smile.

I LIVE HERE, THIS IS MY HOUSE

Listen
I live here
This is my house
If you don't like it
You can get out
I make the rules
And I say what goes
If you don't like it
You can get your clothes
Leave
Vamoose
Yeah that's right
In fact I've had enough
I want you out tonight
Trying to tell me
How the hell I should raise my kids
Well I don't appreciate it anymore
In fact I never did
We had a thing going
A little romance
You moved in
Everything was cool
Then you started
Treating me like I'm still in school

What's wrong with you
Why are you trying to tell me
How to live my life
Last night
I had to tell you five times to…
No
It wasn't twice!
Why are you always lying
You do this all the time
Anyway it doesn't matter
Forget it
I've made up my mind
I want you out
So pack your things
And leave the key
In the little bowl
By the toaster
I don't really care where you go
All I know is it's over
You can go and live with
Those so called friends
You're always going on about
Go and see them
Maybe they can help you out
I'm sure they'll be happy
To put up with you

Telling them
How to live their lives
And what to do
But I live here
This is my house
And I'm not prepared to.

IF POETRY IS A WOMAN

If poetry is a woman
Then tell everyone
I'm seeing someone
And have been for a very long time
That I've had a lot of time to think
And everything
Is going to be just fine

If poetry is a woman
Then tell everyone
The wedding is not off
I've changed my mind
Whether lawfully
Or unlawfully
I take her as my wife
For the rest of my life
To have and to hold
Until death do us part
And that even in death
We will remain together
Inseparable
Just as we were from the start
And that when I die
They'll bury me with my dear poetry

44

In my heart
They'll say his woman was his true love
Among all his works of art

If poetry is a woman
Then I wish
To consecrate the vows now
To only make love to one woman
The same woman
Every night
Or whenever we like
Until our hearts delight
We will be with each other
And speak with each other
About everything
And nothing
We will small talk
And talk deep
About life
And all that we seek
Until we are complete
And if ever she's asleep
I'll write her by candlelight
On vanilla coloured sheets
And there I'll stay
Studying her features

In awe and transfixed
Until daylight dawns
Upon her beauty once again
And she awakens
And arises
Once more
Like a phoenix

If poetry is a woman
Then tell everyone
That I've now got all the answers
To all their questions
About me being in love
And that I'm now
Totally ready for commitment
And that finally
One woman is enough
That I'm a changed man
And that I'll be somewhere
With the wife tonight
Even if they see me
Hanging out at the club
I'll be with her
All the one-night stands
And four week romances
I've given them up

If poetry is a woman
I'm going to raise my daughter
With poetry
So she can grow to see
Exactly how
A woman should be

If poetry is a woman
I'm going to teach my son
How to treat poetry
So he will grow to see
How to treat life
And how life
Is supposed to be

If poetry is a woman
Then you can go ahead
And call off the search
Tell them I've finally found one
I'm going to love
With all that I'm worth
That she will undoubtedly be
My first true love
And that with the things she does
She's got me stuck to her like glue
And hooked like a drug

And no rehabilitation
Is necessary
Required
Welcome
Or wanted
Tell everyone
I said
I rather stay intoxicated
Induced
And under the influence
Of her instead
I can't resist her
I want her
And yes
Her words always go to my head
We lay down
I touch her
She touches me
And yes
I get ink stains all over my bed
But never any regrets

Because if poetry is a woman
With her
I've earned and learned my respect
I adore her every aspect

And if she is calling me to her aid
I will be there to accept
And if she wants me for her slave
I will fetch
Carry and collect
To satisfy her request
With her ball and chain
Around my neck
I promise to
Properly serve and protect
Her interest
To inspire and express
And to stand by her
Regardless of the effects
The only word she won't know
Is neglect
And if anyone
To our union
Should object
We will simply live
Poetically incorrect
Because she fulfils me
And everyday I want more of her
As our relationship grows more beautiful
And more complex
The only things

I've ever really been addicted to
Are poetry
And sex
And the only things
That have ever caused me any real pain
Are poetry
And sex

But if poetry is a woman
Then God knows
The only thing
I'm prepared
To remain faithfully committed to
Is poetry
The only thing I've ever really been able to
Call my own
So what else could one expect
And when they speak of our wedding
They'll say
This is what I said...
I love no other more
Than my beloved poetry
So with this pen
I thee wed.

IN TEARS AND PIECES

A man turns on his TV
Sees a man kidnapped
In a movie
Identical to the way
He saw it happen
To his own wife

It was around this time
Last July
In fact
It was a year ago
Yesterday

He violently
Throws the remote control
At the wall
It breaks into pieces
And falls
As the tears
Fall down his face
The same way
They did that day

It was three weeks ago

In June
When he and a close friend
Had re-organised the house
For a school reunion do

A guest
Looks at a picture
And says
This must be the lovely wife
I can't wait to meet her
Will she be home soon?

INDISCRETIONS

To tell the truth
I've lost count
Of the amount of sexual encounters
But in the end
When all is said and done
What really counts
Is what it all amounts to
Subtract the time taken away
By each night and each day
Minus the cheap thrills
And expensive bills
And it doesn't add up to much
I'm left still counting
On finding the one for me
Take away the sex
And I'd still do it for the company
So what really counts

What it is
To be less young
Less wild and carefree
Still smiling
Less naive
With all that said

I still find myself
Spending time in bed
With women
I really have no business being with
Time that would've been better spent
Being with my kids
But at the same time
Without that
My two offspring wouldn't even exist
Seems every time I cease and desist
Out steps another seductress
On a mission to please and persist
And my addictive personality
Makes good sex
A thing hard to resist
Especially when I mostly get back
Only half as good as I give

I'm like
What type of bad behaviour is this
Slipshoddiness
Sloppiness
Slovenliness
Perhaps therein lies
What the problem is
You never know

What you're going to get
And it's all a little bit
Too hit and miss
How easily we forget
And retrospect
Doesn't appear to be stopping this
Solving this

In my reconnaissance
I've lost sight
Of how many abortions
I've played a part in over time
I've often contemplated
If god is watching
Sees it as murder
And we'll all be tried for our crimes
In this life
With it forever
Weighing on our minds
And in the afterlife
Standing before all the faces
Of the lives we denied
Having to explain why
Why they were forced to die

As said

You never know
What you're going to get
Speaking of which
Death is a high price to pay
Just to get your needs met
Dick wet
Pussy wet
I often say
Unprotected sex with a stranger
Is like a game of Russian roulette
But what's stranger
Is how I all too often
Seem to forget
With each new conquest
Developing a case of amnesia
When it comes to that latex

I told my young teenage son
To save sex
And if you don't son
Make it safe sex
Keep in mind
I'm too young to be a grandparent yet
And so is your mum
Now he's the same age as I was
When I started having fun

And his sister and him
Are only apart by 10 months
So my wise advice
Is like a double contradiction
When looking at my life
And the things that I've done

Maybe I'll be an old romantic
Still believing in love
And that one day it'll come
Maybe I missed it
Maybe I jinxed it
Dismissed it
Well before it begun
Maybe I'm an escapee
Injured
Still hurting
In pain and on the run
Loaded shotgun

Nevertheless
I've just left the boudoir
Of yet another woman
I know in my heart
Isn't the one
And I'm looking back at myself

From the bathroom mirror
Like really?
Is this the greatest we can do
Chasing and impregnating women
Who aren't even in the faintest
Concentrating on you
Talking marriage and babies
When you only just started dating
There's a place
For people as crazy as you

I'm unimpressed
Maybe you'd be better dressed
If you didn't invest yourself so much in sex
The way that you do
In future
Keep your clothes on
Perhaps you'll see less stress
And be able to get more ahead
And progress
The day that you do
And yeah, you say that you do
But from where I'm looking from
Lover boy
I pray that you do.

IT'S ALL ABOUT THE WEAVE

You are my
Weave queen
My weave baby
You're my weave lady
Keep weaving, baby
You got me weave crazy
So please weave for me today see
Don't be lazy
Get your weave on
Come on
You know I love it
Long and strong
So I can hold on all night long
Give me your weave
Not your thong

Afros and cornrows no longer belong
Those days are long gone
Going back to your roots
Well so long
See ya
Better lace up your boots
Wouldn't want to be ya
Because I'm a weave king

Down with the weave thing
Seeing is believing
A weave is most pleasing
Don't want a woman
If she's not weaving
Even the wonderful Stevie
Could see easily
That the girl of my dreams
Is weavy

Weave
Weave
Weave

Work that weave
Wiggle that weave
Wear that weave
Right down to your knees
Instead of world-wide web
Give me world-wide weave
So I can see the streets teaming
With Nubian weave queens
With all colours
Red, gold and green
And blue
Mothers and grandmothers

And babies too
Just weaving the weave way
Let weave lead the way I say

Weavy
Weavy
Weavy

Hip hip hooray

Weavy
Weavy
Weavy

Hip hip hooray

Let it swing
Let it sway
Even if it doesn't fit
Let it stay

Weavy
Weavy
Weavy

Hip hip hooray

Get your weave today
And weave for me, ladies
If you're already weaving
Just keep weaving, baby
I want you all to drive me
Weave
Crazy.

LETTER TO ARGARTHIA

You flow
So
Perfect
And you know
It's worth it
Just to turn up to each show
And watch you
Work it
Slow
Or fast
I have watched you grow
So vast
Within this
Poetry circuit
And I want you to know
It's more
Than just the way you word it
You see
I honestly believed
That if there was anything
Left to hear or see
On this poetry scene
That I had already heard it
But with you

It's the way you assert it
Not just being assertive
Or the way you vindicate the space
But also the way in which
You make your presence felt
Preserving your poetical essence
As though not to do so
Is detrimental to your health
It's essential
You've realised the core of your wealth
Resides inside yourself
You can afford
To be experimental when you recite
I swear
I saw all their pens and pencils
Vanish out of sight
As if they don't write
The last time you touched the mic
I guess they're afraid
That they might
Not seem half as bright
Against your light
And I laugh inside
Every time I witness the fright
That your aura stirs up inside them
You said you lose friends

Every time you do this
And its true
It's like man
Fears what he doesn't understand
Blinded by your gleam
He'll always
Either try to fight
This force he can't conceive
Or back away rejecting it
Not wanting to believe
And she
Is just the same
Maybe even worse
Envious anytime she feels your energies
Or hears your words
She is cursed
By the verbs
And pronouns
You have now found
To be your gown and crown
Which you wear so proud
As you say them loud
Dressing and addressing audiences
With your ordinances
Wrapped around them like shrouds
Mystic

As you unveil their minds
To redesign their spirits
With your lyrics
Some say you're gifted
Others say you're twisted
I say
Just keep me lifted
I don't care
Where your precious soul is going
Or where it's been
I just want to hear you sing
My soul
Into a myriad of feelings
The sexual can't compare
Comes nowhere near
To this kind of healing
You bring
You are a goddess
And I am blessed
Just to hear the whisper of your breath
Much less
The syllables you resurrect
Every time you express
The spirituals
That abide deep inside your chest
I have watched you rise with the best

Just like a phoenix
You wear your success
Around your neck
Where you'll never forget
And where everyone else can see it
You say there's self respect
And there's being conceited
And I believe it
And if half the poets on the scene
Would agree
It would be a nicer place
For you and me to be
You see
Each face I see
Used to tell the same
Old
Story
Until you
Sang your flow
For
Me.

LIKE A THIEF IN THE NIGHT

Like a thief in the night
I creep beneath the moonlight
Seeking the next prey
Who will be my delight
If you're sleeping
Let's say
I could be keeping your wife
Now, you would swear blind
She would never leave the bed
And she's always with you
Most of the time
But the truth is though
I'm the host
When she's sleeping in mine
Once the coast is clear
And she gives the sign
We arrange to meet
Discreet
At a low-key place and time
Not a trace you'll find
Because I'm a master at what I do
You may have your suspicions
But you'll never have proof
Aloof

And way ahead of you
I plan my next hit
I do what I do
And damn I don't give a shit
Because nothing feels sweeter to me
Than another man's property
And besides
I couldn't get my hands on it
If you were looking after it properly
I call it robbery
Of the worst degree
Done most intelligently
And I'm sure if they could put me away
They'd lock me up
Indefinitely
I'm guilty
And can't help myself
From this case of kleptomania
That motivates my moves
If I see her and I like her
I've got to take her
And that's my mood
I pick and choose like food
Tall ones
Fat ones
Short ones

Slim ones
Just got to get in one
And I never lose
Because they never refuse
I use and abuse
Bruise and confuse
Screw and amuse
But you'll never ever catch me
Or know the things I do
Because
Hear the news
I never
Leave clues.

LUSTFUL THINKING

So brazen
And carefree
You approach me
Speaking of love and poetry
Of poetry and love
Not knowing me much
But enough to make a fuss
With your desire for me
To write you
A poem of love
But my mind is preoccupied
With visions of other stuff
Imagining us
Entwined inside a bathtub of lust
Creating music
From the way that we use it
And the way that we touch
It's too much
My libido goes on ahead of me
Making way for thoughts
Of only you
The bed
And me
In my head it seems so heavenly

Like the calm breeze
Received by two
Who lay upon white sand
By blue seas
Between two palm trees
Take my hand
And come go with me
To a land
Where your every fantasy
Becomes a reality
Where no other can challenge me
For once there
I become a burning fire
Burning with desire
To please you
And oh your eyes
Your eyes
They tell me
How much you want me
And how long it's going to be
Before you explode
From yearning and wanting
For my endless love
Which speaks to you
And heats you up
Like sunbeams from above

Just your luck
I love to touch
And caress
Too much say some
But nevertheless
I'm the best
I'll make you succumb
And come
And come
And come
And come
Again
And again
And again
For just a taste of some
Of what you won't be able to resist
Let's have some fun, Miss
The thought of a smooth kiss
From your butter smooth lips
And oh your cool hips
And other bits
Make me want to do some things
And touch you in places
So fine
Your inner thighs
Embrace this

Slim waistline of mine
Inside my mind a thousand times
It's all I can think of
Your love
My love
Our love
Or even no love
Just
Us
You and me together
In lust.

MARIA

I know this girl named Maria
I'd love you to see her
Exceptionally intelligent
Pursues chemistry as her career
She wants to be a pharmacist
She studies university sciences
The kind of girl
That could tell you what time it is
She knows what's what
She'll have you figured out from the off
The kind of girl you see on the street
And just have to stop
And drop a line
About how you think she's fine
And about how maybe the two of you
Could maybe meet up sometime
To maybe wine and dine
You'll feel inclined
She'll blow your mind
With intellectual dialogue
She loves to read books a lot
But still sexy and hot
The kind of girl that you see on cover shots
For magazines

Or even movie screens
Or cheerleading
For big name teams
She's every man's dream
She'll make a cheap dress look supreme
She's just turned nineteen
But to look at her
You'd never know it
Because the simple way she carries herself
Just doesn't show it
I'd give her ten out of ten marks every time
For maturity
That's a lot more marks than the majority
Of these round the way females
With no authority
No focus or no discipline
Try to reach them with a way forward
But they ain't listening
Don't want to think
Rather smoke and drink
And go to the clubs
Not every other weekend
But every other day
Brother, what's that
That's the kind of girl
That'll hold you back

A non-progressive element
That loves idol chit-chat
A good definition of slack
To be exact
The kind of girl
That sleeps around a lot
Lying to all the different men she's got
Switching off her phone
When she's not alone
Far from the kind of girl
I want in my home
I'd rather be on my own
I need a girl like Maria
Each and every woman
With her head screwed on
Wants to be her
She's got the plot right
That's the kind of woman
I want in my life
No strife
We'd make love all night
Under the moonlight
Giving birth to new stars
Under the sky
And they too would grow up
With a piece of the pie inside

And by daylight
They'd continue the fight
To make the world right
There's no better delight
Than a male and female
With positive direction
I need a woman
Who can give me more
Than just an erection
Someone to stimulate my mind
Women like Maria
Are hard to find
Many wouldn't even attempt
The heights that she's climbed
Too scared
To put themselves out there
And stand for something
Can't accept the challenges
Then you stand for nothing
As far as I'm concerned
Respect and success
Are things you earn
Not to mention
Trust
That's what I've learned
And it burns

That so many out there
Waste years
Term to term
Maria just stands firm
Doing what she needs to do
To get through
And she understands education is crucial
So she does everything that's necessary
And useful
Towards the attainment of her goals
She knows the value of knowledge
Is more than silver and gold
God bless her soul
She's got future plans
With all directions mapped out
She still lives at home now
But she's soon to move out
And buy a big house
Somewhere down south
By the sea
She's always loved the ocean
So that's where she wants to be
Living carefree
Away
From the speed of the city.

MILCAH

Just here thinking
What I would like to say to you
What I would like you to know
And it being no word of a lie
I want to be there when you laugh
I want to be there when you cry
Don't try to hide your feelings
Deep down inside
I'm dealing with your soul
Your body and your mind
You said you want me deeper
Well now is the time
We said no matter what
This vibe we wouldn't prescribe
I'm in a situation
But I believe we can still fly
Why kill this high
Why let it die
What a thrill this ride
If we get it right
I say no hook-ups
No hang-ups
But why should I make love to you
If I can't make you mine

And vice versa
Because I know you see the signs
Should we embark
On this mountainous journey
If we're unsure we can climb
Should we cross this bridge
Should we throw caution to the wind
If we're unsure we can finish
Should we begin.

MOVIE STAR

Baby wants to be a movie star
Fine clothes and fancy cars
Spend money in expensive bars
Champagne and caviar
Fly far to all the nice places
Take pictures with famous faces
Diamond necklaces
Diamond bracelets
Turn up to premieres
Looking outrageous
Sign autographs
Next day she's in the papers
Paparazzi
Catching all her sexy capers
Shameless

She says, after all
Who could blame us
No-one really wants
To live and die nameless
I say, go ahead, baby
Do ya thing
Be famous
Go ahead, baby

Be famous

She's into magazine covers
And latest fashions
New designer shoes
And handbag matching
She's like show me the money
Show me the action
Ain't got time for it
If it ain't happening
Want to get with her
You better meet satisfaction
No class or style
You are not her passion
Better have it going on
Or you're just a distraction

She's appointment at 6
But can fit you in
That's 20 minutes before
She leaves for the gym
It's in her business interest
To keep herself trim
This screen star to be
Must stay the in thing
And that includes hair

Nails and skin
And all the places
Girl is seen in
On her pursuit for loot
And extravagant things

Checked out the hotel
At the airport checking in
She said, the first thing she'd buy
Is a pair of wings
So she could fly
Without the aggravation
Says, standing in line
Is so frustrating
Miss busy body
Is so impatient
Likes being waited on
But doesn't like waiting

Swoops down on you like a hawk
For procrastinating
No delaying
And no hesitating
If she doesn't like your talk
She'll be saying
And from the way she walks

You'll know she ain't playing
She's like
I've got to be somewhere
So don't waste my time
Coming round here
If you ain't prepared
To take me there

She's busy on the phone
Getting her hair made
Dinner date at eight
Can't be late
She said
I know its Sunday
But tell the lord he can wait
Because church mass
Ain't paying my way
Does god know
Who I have to meet today?

Baby wants to be a movie star
Fine clothes and fancy cars
Spend money in expensive bars
Champagne and caviar
Fly far to all the nice places
Take pictures with famous faces

Diamond necklaces
Diamond bracelets
Turn up to premieres
Looking outrageous
Sign autographs
Next day she's in the papers
Paparazzi
Catching all her sexy capers
Shameless

She says, after all
Who could blame us
No-one really wants
To live and die nameless
I say, go ahead, baby
Do ya thing
Be famous
Go ahead, baby
Be famous.

MYSTICAL AUTHENTIC PERFECTION

And there I was
Feeling vibed out
And ready for a night out
I walked up to the club
Where couples were queuing up
With single women in fours
And brothers hoping to score for sure
I could hear the DJ playing
So the band were still setting up
You see
I love live music
And can't get enough
Started singing along to the song
Finally I came to the door
Paid my five and went inside
Felt the eyes on me
But ignored
I went downstairs
Clive and Seymour were there
Drinking and joking
About some woman's hair
Didn't care
I looked around
Glad to see a few faces that I knew

Saw a lot more that I didn't
But that was cool too
The band started to play
And the host came out
Singing, Killing Me Softly
But some people were blocking me
So I moved to where I could see properly
She sang another two songs
Then she announced the first artist
She came on stage to perform
And that's where it all started
It was more than mystical
The way she grabbed the mic device
And with a voice smooth like chocolate
Proceeded telling my whole life
It was nice
With an authenticity
That could only be known to me
Indeed she had a perfection
It seemed that only I could see
And the way that she moved
To and fro
Up and down the stage
Had me feeling so many ways
I was in a daze
Amazed

From the way
That she handled the vocal melody
I became her patient
And she became my remedy
She definitely
Had the counteractive for me
The medicine
The cure
The antidote
And the relief
She had me hot
But please
I didn't want her to stop
This is Hip hop
I wanted her to carry on
Singing her song
All night long
Until everyone else was gone
Don't give a damn if I'm right or wrong
This is where she belongs
Doing what I believe
She was divinely made for
Singing so sweet
So raw and hard-core over the beat
So precise
And so complete

So expressive and unique
Who's going to step up and compete
After this one
To me she's second to none
I've seen so many come
And only some
Get the job half done
And at first
I was unsure of her intentions
But she's taken me into heights
And dimensions
Way too much
To mention.

NO LYE

Now remember, ladies
It's no lie
See
Your afro hair
Is really alright by me
Yes
Oh how I love
Those precious curls you have
Or had
Come on, girls
Let's go back
The fact is
Your hair
Doesn't really look good to us like that
And any man that disagrees
Is obviously under the same spell
That causes you to commit that act
Oh, but it's much more manageable
Yeah
Like hell it is
What chemical processing
Could be more manageable than this
I hope your scalp
And hair follicles

Think so in a few years
Yeah, yeah
I know about hair
I know about the cuticle
The cortex
The medulla
Do you really think it's alright
To put that stuff in there
It's poison
Get to know
Be aware
Don't say
You don't care
As long as your hair looks good
As long as your hair's done
The long term effects of that stuff
Can cause a lot of harm
And it really will be done
If you don't start listening
And taking note
And stop taking it for a joke
Because you'll have no hair left
Remember a head of hair
Can only take so much stress
But maybe you're all trying to be bald
Or maybe there's something I don't know

But as far as I can see
You crucify your good hair
And then wonder why it won't grow
Bleach the life out of it
Then wonder why
You can't get a nice shine out of it
If your hair was supposed to lie down
Like other races
Then it would
But instead, it stood
And grew up towards the sun
The way it should
And oh my sister
You were so beautiful
And looked so good
What a shame
What happened to you
What happened to us
They washed our brains
So now we apply the lye
The l-y-e
Will it wash away
Maybe
But not until
We wash away
The l-i-e's

Now, my sisters
This is not a diss
I hope you'll see
This
Is just a message
And a plea.

NOBODY'S PROPERTY

You want to lock me up
But I'm not your property
You want to treat me as your own
But that's not treating me properly
You hate to think
You have to share me with the world too
But we both know
They too
Deserve all the goodness I've given you
All the good vibes
And all the conversation
We both know
Is like food to a hungry nation
You would rather starve them
Than part with a piece of your pie
Your selfishness
Wants to put me away
So much
Until it makes you cry
But I can never be just yours
That's not the way
It was meant to be
You shouldn't cage a bird
That was born to be free

For it will never feel comfortable
Inside the nest you build
Knowing that it doesn't come and go
Of its own free will
One day you may let it out to fly
And it may not come home
And that will be the day
You will say
If only I had known
That this little bird
Was not my property
And that treating it as my own
Was not treating it properly.

PRINCESS IN A BLACK FACE

Elegant
Prestigious
And avant-garde
Yes, that indeed she is
Without a doubt
Authoritativeness and subtlety
Are only some among the qualities
Her aura sends out
So intelligent and wise is she
That even the most knowledgeable
Must humble
Fools often scorn
The wisdom of her words
Only to fall and stumble
Her greatness is matched by few
But aspired for by many
A woman of her calibre
I have never yet met any
She's a true winner
But it seems
She'll never even be given
A chance to run the race
Princess
In a black face

She's the mother of civilisation
Who gave birth to the first children
She gave them love and wisdom
And everything else
Necessary to build them
She has a powerful mind
Capable of leading nations
Countries
And sovereign states
But still with a soft spot
For animals
Trees
Rivers
And landscapes
She's in tune with nature
And every good thing
It has to offer mankind
She wants to make major contributions
To change and save our world
From future decline
And that's fine
But within this society
It seems
She'll never reach her desired place
Princess
In a black face

She's a ghetto superstar
By far without question
She's a girl for the new world
With no second guessing
She makes the sunlight shine
On hearts where there is rain
She creates much joy there
Where there is pain
With her head firmly on her shoulders
And feet firmly on the ground
There is not a truer woman
Who deserves her crown
She has a recipe for success
That I truly hope one day
She will receive the pleasure to taste
Because it would be a waste
Princess
In a black face.

RESCUE ME

Now that's my kind of speed dating
No waiting
No hesitating
No debating
And no faking
Don't see me somewhere
Be attracted to me
Want to talk to me
But then decide
You're not going to approach me
Because you're the female
That's so old fashioned
Don't get me wrong
I'm kind of an old fashioned dude
But show me something new
You approach me
And start the action
That's what to do
I've witnessed so many women
On the street
And at clubs
And other places
Just blow a guy right out so bad
Like she was just getting ready to slap him

I see that
And just be taking a step back
Relaxing
So unless you're approaching me
It's not going to be happening
And a lot of the time
You liked the guy
Before he even made his move
So what are you doing?
Stop acting
That to me
Is so unattractive
So unhealthy
So do the right thing
Set yourself free
Set me free
Let it go
Let's go get sexy
You know
I respect you
And you respect me
Don't be like the others
Come and get me
Rescue me
Let me rescue you
That's the best you could do

It doesn't matter
That I just met you
Pretend there's no-one else
In the room but me
And just express you
Show me attitude
Not the kind
That makes you put up your guard
But the type that lets you
Show me
That you wouldn't be afraid
To take all your clothes off
And just throw them on the floor
Because in my mind
I would've already undressed you
A thousand times
And seen it all before
Long before you caught me
Looking at your thighs
While you were sitting at the bar
With your lips on that straw
Sipping and licking on it seductively
Because you knew I was watching
So you did it some more
And at first I wasn't certain
If you were really flirting

But what did it for sure
Is when you passed me
On your way to the bathroom
With your girls
And whispered in my ear you were bored
Making it clear
You weren't in the mood
For just innocently kicking lyrics
And trying to build a rapport
Instead you came out to be found
Go missing
Have fun and explore
And I too wasn't just out to network
Listen and talk
Because I just came back from promoting
And spitting lyrics on tour
And long before anyone knew it
We were busy
Slipping out the door
Slipping into your home
Slipping in a CD by Joe
Or Jodeci
Who knows
We're sipping on drinks
We slip into kissing
Slipping out of our clothes

Slipping into bed
I slip you into surprise
Slip you into a zone
As I slide my tongue
Just where you want it to go
I'm slipping into your mind
Slipping into your bones
So much so that you forget
To send a text through
To let your girls know
You won't need to be rescued
Unlike last time
When they left you
At the club with some guy
You didn't want to be next to
You breathe in
Exhale
And smile
Like you're pleased to have me
Next to you
To have me undress you
Caress
And sex you
Right round until the next morning
When the driving instructor calls in
To collect you

But the phone is off the hook
So he can't connect to you
So he decides to knock the door
But is stopped by the sounds of you
Screaming out
Like someone's distressing you
But it's not
It's me
Still pleasuring you
So what does he do
Calls the police
Like you would expect him to
You're annoyed and yelling
Why now
But my question to you
Is why didn't he eavesdrop a little longer
To conclude
That you didn't need the rescue
And you look at me
Smile
And cut your eyes
In that sexy style that expresses you
Then you turn and say
If they knew
What a freak you turned me into
Last night

They'd have arrested you
And I laugh and say
Yeah
It's true
But some fine sexy young thing
Provided the inspiration for that
Guess who
And we laugh about it some more
While laying up
Watching the rest of the news
Finally falling asleep
Until three
In your single bed for two
Mumbling
That the sex was the best
And very spiritual
Saying, bless you
For coming to my rescue.

S.T.E.P F.O.R.W.A.R.D

She talks esoteric parables
Focusing on rectifying worlds
Altering reality's destiny

Against her will
She gave birth
To the twisted underground
Her mind now like spaghetti junction
She feeds on alphabet porridge
To increase her knowledge function
Souping up her faculties capacity
Through suction
Soaking up the answers to her existence
Practising reverse mind abduction

Separating nonsense

From a world that spins triangle
In rectangular heptagons
Pinpointing the source
To its blueprint of confusion
And the fountainhead
Of its candy coated
Created illusion

But first

She had to sacrifice
The soft and tender parts of her heart
Temporarily amputated them
From her thinking
Making her third eye more receptive
So she could see the future's future
And alter it via its past
Manipulating the gift of prognosis
To assist her purpose

She now

A psyche sorceress
A sorcerous soothsayer
Her voice like sign language
Prophesying
Revealing the signs of the times

To come

Subconsciously transforming her body
Into a vessel
To deliver verbal projectiles
Whilst trying to reopen senses

To deeply imbed her ideals
And inject her effigy
Of the way things are
And how everything should be
Orally drilling into the coffin
Of dead spirits
In order to resurrect them mentally
With her lyrics
Provoking souls to proliferate
With renewed perception
And insight

But first

She had to momentarily
Paralyse her weaker emotions
So she could gain strength
From hard times
And become an elixir to her plight

Her pain and her fame
Can be found deep woven
Into intellect cities
Or entangled in decision crossroads
Her walk is parabolic Jesus fashion
Her step is forward

But before she could step forward

She had to step back
Backwards
Walking the hardships of the hard-line
Like a tightrope
Above a pit of sleeping heads
Taking precautions
Not to fall back
Fall back in her thinking
For the fate of tomorrow's sun people
Sits burning indelibly
At the back of her eyes

She talks esoteric parables
Focusing on rectifying worlds
Altering
Reality's
Destiny.

SAY MY NAME

There, I said it
Now just calm down
And forget it
You really need to stop
Feeling so insecure
Because everyday
I want you
More and more
I love you
I want to be with you
I need you
So what's the deal?
Tell me how that feels
I'm keeping it real
Later we'll go for a meal
But if it makes you happy
I'll say your name
Just to show you, baby
Ain't nothing changed
Everything's still the same
Let me say it again
Just to ease your brain
Loving you, baby
Is my only aim.

SENSUOUS

Creeping out
From the shadows
Into the morning after the night before
She finds herself
An inner love divine
A woman's world
A brighter side
As she now flies high
Like the birds
No longer caught up in delusion
For she had met his kind
A thousand times
He who knew how to play on her mind
And on the many truths
Her heart had spoken
How to play on her emotions
And use them as tokens
To keep her open
Long enough for him to keep playing
Knowing
He would leave her
Broken
Soaking in her tears
Hoping she would soon discover one

Who would come and erase the pain
In her years
The pain
That came through mans struggle
To prove his masculinity
The hurt that came through a friend
Victim to her own selfish desires
And helpless vanity
And the regret
That stemmed from her own calamity
And temporary insanity
In the midst of illusionary love
Love that never was
Love that never would be
She began to see
That these previous
Tried and tested methods
With the wrong lovers
Suggested that she was
Best with being strong within herself
Before others
She glances at her reflection
In the stillness of the water
Honouring her skin
Silky and smooth
A sun-kissed satura

Of cinnamon and sepia
As she serenely sings
Sweet soulful symphonies
As soothing as a septet
Served by seven seraphs
So solemn
Sonorous
And sincere
Her sleek sound
Slowly softens
And serenades the senses
Once a captive of her sensuality
This now prima donna
Causes serendipity to see its inabilities
And be envious
For she is now queen of her destiny
Ruler over her heart and senses
For she is now
Sensuous.

SHE

She came to me
In the broad light of days
Time told me her name
By nights
She was a sent princess
She told me my name would be Prince

Because
Personal realisation
is necessary
concerning elevation

P.R.I.N.C.E

Because
Personal Realisation
Is Necessary
Concerning Elevation

She smiled her light on me
And told me
If I wanted her to
She would stay with me
For the rest of eternity.

SUSIE'S BAKERS

Anytime you came there
You could be guaranteed
There she would be
Stacking a shelf
Sweeping the floor
Tidying up
Serving customers
Or just behind the counter
Waiting to greet you
As you came in to buy something
She was a very diligent young woman
Articulate
And very dedicated to her work
I had often heard people
Address her as Miss Jennings
Whenever they came into the store
Others would often address her as Susie
Which was also the name on the shop sign
Leading me to realise
That this business
She so enthusiastically preserved
And maintained
Was her own
Such an achievement

For someone so young
I would always think to myself
Anytime I came by
And there was always
A constant reminder
Of her growth
Success
And the respect
She had managed to build up
Within the community
It was an honour
Seeing her business develop
And expand over the years
And it was a joy
To hear the delivery van
Coming through our way in the evenings
To deliver bread and cakes
To the homes in our neighbourhood
And to look out of the window
And see people
Coming out of their houses
Hurrying across the green to buy some
On the side of the van
It said, Susie's Bakers
And that was a beautiful thing
That was a beautiful thing.

TONIGHT'S THE NIGHT

Late night
Candle light
The vibes right
Tonight
We won't fight
Tonight
We're going to do it right
Courteous
Warm
Polite
Showing nuff love
Sometimes, honey
We cuss too much
Don't ya think
Less talking
And more touch
Is what we need
To make this love feel
More relevant than the TV
Switch that off
Play a CD
Something soft
Like Jo-Jo and K-Ci
No Jay-Z

118

Maybe
Dru Hill or The Isley's, baby
I'll leave it up to you
To surprise me, baby
Because you're my lady
And I know you'll come through
With the right groove
And a little later
That nice food
To put me in the right mood
For loving you
The whole night through
Let's do the things
We used to do
Like take hot bubble baths together
And outside it's cold weather
So I'm sure we'd appreciate the pleasure
And I could rub the back of your neck
And your shoulders
While you rub mine
Relax back in the tub
And forget the time
You say you got worries on your mind
But tonight
Everything will be fine
I've got your favourite

The famous humus dip
With tortilla chips
How's that sound
With the hot chocolate
And crunchy bits
On top of it
I know you like a lot of it
So I brought some more
From the corner store
And of course
How could I forget
Avocado and soy sauce
No sweat
What's next
I'm at your request
Come and take a seat, baby
Rest your feet
No stress
Just you and me
The way we're supposed to be
Tonight I need you close to me
So tell me honestly
What's it going to be
I want you
Do you want me?

TRYING TO REACH MY SISTER

I'm trying to reach my sister
But it's obvious she isn't there
Or maybe she can hear me
But doesn't really care
I just wanted to say a few things to her
Been text messaging her
Been paging her
Surely by now
She must have recognised the caller ID
She's probably
Ignoring the calls I'm sending
Switched off
And it wouldn't surprise me
She always said I moaned too much
Going on and on
Preaching
About how she should live her life
But she was only thirteen then
And carrying a knife
Now she's fifteen
Acting and thinking she's big
Going on fifty
But the reality is
She's young

And mum thinks she'll listen to me
Well I really hope so
Because right now
It doesn't look too good
I just don't seem to be getting through
She thinks she's a grown woman now
So she does what she wants to do
She thinks that selling drugs
Is the way to build a secure future
And the way to survive
Is carry a gun
In case someone tries to shoot ya
Most girls
Most smart girls her age
Are still in school
Learning
You know
Having fun
Doing the things that young girls do
But no
She's a mother
At almost sixteen
And soon to be a mother of two
People say it's the upbringing
But in our house
It was just our mum

And I can tell you
She did nothing less than her best
Could've been
The lack of a father figure I guess
But nevertheless
Somewhere it all went wrong
Got pregnant for a drug dealer
Nearly twice her age
And a little after that time
She was gone
They stayed in Swiss Cottage somewhere
And did business back and forth
Overseas from there
But apparently they got some information
The house was under surveillance
And decided to disappear
They stayed low for a few months
And sent the children away
To his mother's in Canada for a while
So they could easily travel a lot more
They thought it was best
To travel as light as possible
As of course
They could never be sure
I've managed to keep in touch with her
Despite her constant business trips abroad

And changing of her number
Me and mum can only wonder when
And wait for the day
It all goes under
Because it's not long
Until this drug fast life
Comes to a sudden halt
And all the money
And luxuries
Are gone down the drain
And the parents face the prison sentence
While the children bear the strain
And without proper parental guidance
In order to create a change
The cycle doesn't alter
But simply remains the same
And if you were killed
Or went to prison
It would send mum to her grave
And I myself I love you
And I just couldn't bear the pain
So I'm trying to reach you sister
And I know you're really there
I know that you can hear me
But I really hope you care.

WAKE UP, HONEY

Wake up honey
There's someone at the door
He said we've wasted a lot of time
But we can't afford to waste anymore
He said he's been knocking all morning
He's obviously very persistent
He said he's come to bring us a message
That'll help us if we listen
He said we've got to get ready now
Otherwise we'll be late
Opportunity is at the door with him
But he's saying it won't wait
He said the time is now
Success is around the corner
Waiting up the road on the high street
He said the reason why he's here
Is so that we all could meet
We must arise now he says
And seize the day with all its eminence
Rendering all past thoughts of failure
Non-productive and irrelevant
Releasing all fears
And welcoming every challenge
Every gauntlet thrown down

He says tomorrow is ours for the taking
If only we take it now
So wake up, honey, let's go
Let's get a move on
He says success awaits us
But if we don't hurry it'll be gone
And we'll be left to wallow
And cascade in the memory
Of what could have been
He said imagine the pain we would feel
If we let this go
It's an awful scene
He showed me examples of so many
Who have abandoned
And forsaken their aspirations
When all that was missing
Was focus and discipline
Along with self application
He said quitters will never win a thing
Because they quit
Before their ship comes in
I said what do you mean?
He said they give up their dreams
They try hard but not hard enough
So they give up the idea of achieving
They see no immediate success

So they cease believing
He took this picture from his pocket
And showed me
What the future could be
I was quite surprised
As it was a picture I've never seen
Of you and me
It shows us
In our most courageous
And resourceful states
It shows we have all we need within us
And we don't have to wait
So wake up, honey
There's much to be done
And procrastination
Isn't doing us any favours
So you get yourself prepared, honey
As quickly as you can
And I'll go and wake the neighbours.

WE SHALL DANCE

Yesterday
It was vintage wine and fine food
In a candlelit night
Today we dance away
Under the beams of a cool moonlight
Can't take my eyes off you
So beautiful
The way you move
And the things you do
The way you groove
Fine red dress
Fine hair
And fine shoes
You know, baby
You move with the essence of a true lady
Take you anywhere in this world
If you dance for me
They say I'm crazy
But that's because
They haven't seen the way
In which you captivate me
I'm living la vida loca lately
And I used to have friends
But now they hate me

Because I'm with you
Envious
Passing by with their jealous eyes
At the things we do
Telling lies
Wishing they were me
So they could be with you
But those lies are see-through
Can't see your heart
They need a key to
Me without you
Is like the nut
Without the screw
And I've got nothing to prove
Only you to lose
And who knows
Later on in life I may take a chance
Make that step
And let a love enhance
But for right now
By the shower of a moonlit fountain
We shall dance
We dance by the Pyramids
We dance by the Sphinx
We dance by the great China wall
And all those things

You elevate me
But at the same time
You send me frantic
Whoever thought
Me and you would cruise the Atlantic
That I would bring you
The finest flowers
Handpicked
We laughed
When I nearly fell in the sandpit
That kiwi juice
You couldn't stand it
Got sick for two days
And I couldn't handle it
Then on the ship
The baby alligator escaped
You sighted it
And gave chase
Never met a woman as brave
As you
Never seen a man change
The way you changed me, boo
That's the truth
Then from that
We flew
To view the Nazca Lines of Peru

Footprints in the sand
You take my hand gladly
Saying you don't know what you'd do
If you didn't have me
We make each others fantasy
Become a reality
In France
On the balcony
Overlooking the city
And we dance.

WESTSIDE SUZIE

We don't understand
We warned you
About Westside Suzie
So excuse me
If we're a little confused
To see you and her
Cruising the street
Like everything's sweet
And to hear now that the reason
You haven't been around us
Is because you've been kicking it with her
For the past few weeks
You're a grown man
Of course
Do what you want to do
See who you want to see
But we specifically warned you
To stay away from Westside Suzie
She's bad news
Remember that?
You remember us saying that, right?
I know you remember me saying that
You remember the little rhyme?

She's a beauty
A real cutie with a booty
But what would better suit me
Is to stay away
From Westside Suzie
That's my duty...

You remember?
What happened?
You forgot, huh?
You stared at her too long
Turned your dick into stone
Don't you worry though
You're not alone
Many a man hath passed this way
And had the same price to pay
We can't blame you
She's good
Real good
We all got stung by her at some point
During our moment of weakness
Lured into her honey pot
And got hooked on its sweetness
But seriously
We did warn you though
You needed to take heed

It wasn't a joke
We were telling you because we know
Westside Suzie is a no go
What did you expect
A few weeks ago
You didn't even smoke
You look like a wreck
Place is a mess
You look stressed, bro
Guess there's no need to say
We said so
And how long
Have you been wearing those clothes?
You know
The thing with girls like Suzie
Is to make sure you never get close
Enough to have to think about letting go
It's like the moth to the flame scenario
You're attracted to the flame
But if you get too close
You burn
That's how it goes
I suppose
The good thing about this is
That now you know
And so

Hopefully
You'll make better choices next time
Maybe listen to the voices next time
Perhaps listen to your boys next time
We know all about Westside Suzie
We know what she can do
And what she gets up to
What you're telling us isn't new
What do you think we do?
Just speak for the sake of speaking?
We know all about her sneaking
And her creeping
Secret keeping
Secret meetings
What she gets up to on weekends
We told you
But you wouldn't believe then
Everything you're telling us now
We already know
Accessing the pin number
To your voicemail
On your mobile phone
Listening to all your messages
Calling back all the females
She thinks you might be messing with
Finding out who you got on the side

Who you've already slept with
Pressuring them for their address
So she can pay them a visit
So they can sit down
And talk women shit
And what happens then
8 times out of 10
Is this
Whatever you had with the other girl
No matter how innocent
Is finished
Because she doesn't need
That kind of headache
I mean
As a female
I wouldn't want some other female
Calling me up and spoiling my day
Asking me
How do I know him
Where do I know him from
I mean
Who needs that kind of play
I too would just step away
Oh don't get me started on Westside Suzie
Snooping around like an inspector mouse
Turning up unannounced

And unexpected at your house
Talking about
I thought you said you were going out

Yes, I did
And I'm back
So what now?
Private Investigator
Miss Marple
Columbo
Jessica Fletcher
Magnum, P.I.

Remember when she was seeing that guy
From Footlocker
The one who gave us
The pool party VIP passes
And she sent that sexy girlfriend of hers in
The one with the short hair and tight jeans
To flirt with him
And ask about the sports bra
Or what ever it was
And she was making sexual innuendos
And got him to write down his number
And take hers
And told him to call her

On his lunch break
And when he called
Suzie answered the phone instead
That's Westside Suzie, my friend
Stay away
How about
When she was with that rapper guy
And he caught her licking her lips
At the model guy at the fashion show
And he finished with her
Then a couple days later
Out of sheer anger
And frustration
She called the police
And made up a story
That he stole something from her house
And had him arrested
And locked up in a police cell all day
I know you must remember that
Seeing all those police outside
Looking across the street at us
Waiting for us to react
Just asking for a reason
To sling on the silver bangles
Open up the meat wagon
And throw us in the back

Because these days
It's still like that if you're black
So before we further realise that fact
We fall back
And let Suzie be
Let her cruise the streets
For another as naive
As we used to be
Because truthfully
Karma is a bitch
And drama is for TV
And there's plenty
Of stress free
Fish in the sea
The less we see
Of Westside Suzie
The better for you
The better for me
Come on
Let's get you and this place cleaned up.

WORD TO MY SISTERS

Sisters
Stand tall
Because your playing small
Doesn't save our world, girl
We need you
To release those fears and shine
Dry your tears and climb
We're going to make it this time
We just haven't really been trying
We've been shrinking
So others won't feel insecure
Hope it lifts you up to know
You don't have to do that anymore
Inside your mind
Let these words paint an open door
And on the other side
Everything you've been hoping for
See clearly now
All the things that can be
Aiming for the top
No longer settling for plan B
But persevering
Through this life of continuous warfare
And staying calm and collected

Make methods
Both efficient and effective
Staying highly selective
When it comes to an objective
Always dealing with the corrective

Sisters
Stand tall
Even though this struggle for life
Is like a maze of mayhem
Every time you think
You've reached the end
It turns out to be another bend
Towards yet another dead end
Again and again
I know it seems the same
But stay strong
Learn to gain strength
From the length of the pain
And move on
This road is long
But I'll share your load
Until the strain
Of your ball and chain is gone
You can do no wrong
Fighting for what is right

Give me your hand
And we can make it
Through the stormy night
Now don't take it the wrong way
I'm not trying to be your lover
It's just that in this type of struggle
Every sister needs a brother
Blood or no blood
Just someone she can turn to
A responsible man
Who's willing to learn too

Sisters
Stand tall
Because you're blessed
And even thought
We haven't been the best at all
There's still some of us men left
That'll be there
When your back is against the wall
And before most men could crawl
It was a woman who was there
By their side
So now
How could they forsake a woman
Going through hard times

I feel inclined
To release the thoughts of my mind
Always was taught to speak up
And waste no time
I hope one day we'll find
All sisters standing tall
All over the world
Whether women or girls
All are precious pearls
So whether young or old
Take control and shine bold
And worry not
What the future holds
Only mould
And safeguard your souls
Sisters
Stand tall.

YOU

If only words could express
The extent
To which this deep river inside me
Flows for you
I'd be halfway
To a completed picture
In your mind
Of all the beautiful emotions
You have brought me through
To be in your presence
Is truly more than any treasure
In all this vast earth
Truly more than all my dreams
Of all the splendours of the universe
Your scintillating sterling heart
Shines through you
Like the very sun
That permeates the clouds
I'm moved when you speak aloud
But carried
On even the slightest whisper
From your mouth
For having to concentrate
Just that little bit more

On your utterances
Assist me
In my quest to know you
Due to you
I see sides of myself
That no other has seen
But I'm willing to show you
Because you are the one
Who compels me
Towards the pinnacle
Of my highest self
Your closeness is the next best thing
To that of my creator
Indeed there is no one else
Who for me can shine
Quite the way you shine
I'm yet to meet another being
With such a splendid mind
To call you strong
And beautiful
Yet modest
Would be merely
Understatements of your name
Virtuosity and valour
Are within your character
But are understatements

Just the same
You proliferate my thoughts
Into prolonged gazes
Into time and space
Pondering the joys of what it is
To reach the very core of your heart
And find a place
Within the brilliance of your eyes
I see lucidity
In past, present
And future things
Just listening to you
Is as transcendent
As when a nightingale sings
I wish to bless
All the energies of creation
That were required
In order to have brought forth
Your meek and humble soul to me
I wish to continually be in your presence
Eternally
Burning resplendently
As your everlasting flame of positive light
Together we can combine
Igniting a blazing inferno
Adding passion

And excitement
To a star filled night
Only truth
Can shine this bright
And my truth is
I always want you in my life
You see
I'm caught in your aura
And continuously
Captivated by your style
For your peaceful spirit
Radiates you
And flows beguilingly
Like the waters of the Nile
And if only words could express
The extent
To which this deep river inside me
Flows for you
I'd be halfway
To a completed picture
In your mind
Of all the beautiful emotions
You have brought me through
Thank you.

ABOUT THE AUTHOR

Phoenix James is an award winning Writer, Poet, Author and Spoken Word Recording Artist. He began performing his poetic words live on stages across the UK in 1998. His debut spoken word poetry album, *The A.R.T.I.S.T,* was released in 2000. His first limited edition printed collection of poetry, *To Whom It May Concern,* was published in 2003. He has toured and performed his poetry internationally since 2004. He has appeared in films, on television and radio shows, and collaborated with other artists, singer-songwriters, actors, musicians, filmmakers and producers. In 2013, he wrote, directed and produced the feature length mock documentary film, *Love Freely but Pay for Sex.* Phoenix James has written, recorded and released several spoken word poetry albums including, *Phenzwaan Now & Forever* (2009), *A Patchwork Remedy for A Broken Melody* (2020), *FREE* (2021), *Haven for the Tormented* (2021), *With All That Said* (2022), and *Remixes* Volumes: 1 & 2 (2022).

If you enjoyed reading this book, please leave a review online. The author reads every review and they help new readers discover his work.

PHOENIX JAMES

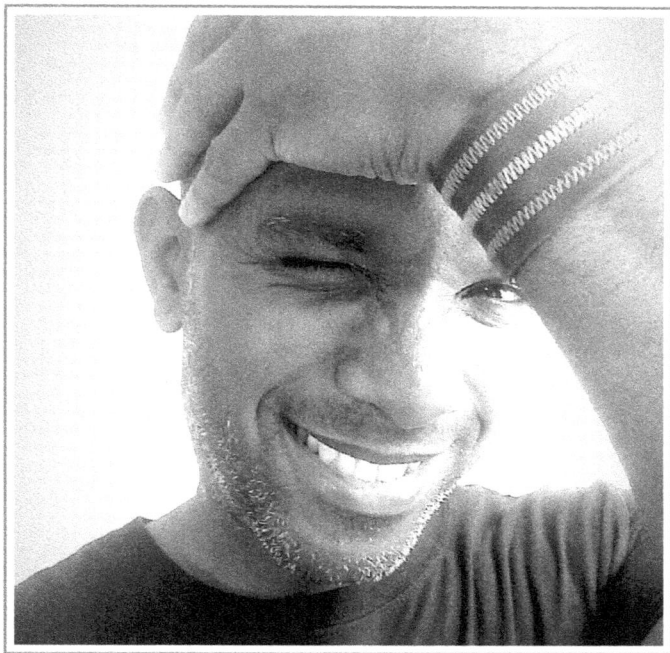

Photo by Phoenix James

Phoenix James lives in London, England.

Connect with Phoenix James on his online social media platforms via www.linktr.ee/ Phoenix_James and say you've read this book. To contact or learn more about Phoenix James and his creative journey or to receive updates via his Newsletter Mailing List, visit his official website at www.PhoenixJamesOfficial.com

Phoenix James Official